Basic Bible Studies

Basic Bible Studies

by Francis A. Schaeffer

TYNDALE HOUSE PUBLISHERS
Wheaton, Illinois

Other Books by Francis A. Schaeffer

Escape from Reason
The God Who Is There
Death in the City
Pollution and the Death of Man
The Church at the End of the Twentieth Century
The Mark of the Christian
The Church Before the Watching World
True Spirituality
He Is There and He Is Not Silent
Genesis in Space and Time

Cover photograph by Jean-Pierre Landenberg

Library of Congress Catalog Card Number 72-81228
ISBN 8423-0103-8

First printing, May, 1972.

Printed in the United State of America.

CONTENTS

I. GOD

II. GOD'S DEALING WITH MAN

III. SALVATION

IV. THINGS OF THE FUTURE

INTRODUCTION

These twenty-five basic Bible studies are meant to give an understanding of the whole *system* of teaching given in the Bible. Very often when people begin to study the Scripture, they do not see the relationship of all its parts. However, because one of the wonderful things about the Bible is its unity, Bible study without keeping this unity in mind is a real loss.

Thus, each individual lesson should be studied with the table of contents consciously in mind, so that each lesson can be seen in relationship to the whole Bible's teaching.

These twenty-five studies are not meant to be read as a book. If they were, a much more detailed text would have been given. Rather, they are to be followed to be a help in a study of the Bible itself. When one begins to go through these studies, he should have both the Old and New Testaments at hand.

Usually, the best way to use these studies is to look up each individual verse in the Bible, to read the verse with care, and then to read the statement which is made in the studies about that verse. The statements are not supposed to be complete explanations of any of the verses. Instead they point out one specific thing that is taught in the verse, as that one specific thing bears on the teaching of that particular lesson. For example, the first Bible reference given

(Ephesians 1:4) has many rich things in it which are not mentioned in the statement following it. But attention is called to just one of the things that Ephesians 1:4 teaches — that God, being a personal God, thinks. Thus, each verse should be looked up and considered in the light of the statement that immediately follows it — not merely as an isolated statement but in the light of that whole lesson, and in the light of the flow of the unity of the biblical teaching as it is set forth in the complete twenty-five studies. The Bible is not just an unrelated group of verses. It is a unit. And it has content that can be studied as one studies other books.

Studied in this way, the Bible will be seen to have many things to say in answer to the questions which men are asking in our generation about the meaning and purpose of life. It tells us who man is, man's purpose, the source of man's problems and the solution to those problems. Of course, this study is just a beginning to help us to begin studying the Bible. The Bible is a unit and eventually we should read it all and see the relationship of each part to the whole. The unity of the Bible begins at the beginning, Genesis, and goes to the end, the book of Revelation.

It is not necessary to do a whole study at a time. If desired, one may spend a specific amount of time each day. When that time is reached, simply draw a line and start at that point the next day.

It would be my advice that each time you do these studies, you speak to God and ask him to give you understanding through the use of the Bible and the study together. If someone pursues these studies who does not believe that God exists, I would suggest that you say aloud in the quietness of your room: "O God, if there is a God, I want to know whether you exist. And I ask you to make me willing to bow before you if you do exist."   —Francis A. Schaeffer

I. GOD

1 / THE GOD OF THE BIBLE

The God of the Bible is personal.

Ephesians 1:4 Notice here that God has a plan, that he thinks.

Genesis 1:1 God not only thinks; he acts.

John 3:16 God not only thinks and acts, God feels. Love is an emotion. Thus the God who exists is personal. He thinks, acts, and feels, three distinguishing marks of personality. He is not an impersonal force, nor an all-inclusive everything. He is personal. When he speaks to us, he says "I" and we can answer him "you."

Deuteronomy 6:4 The Old Testament teaches there is only one God.

James 2:19 The New Testament also teaches there is only one God.

But the Bible also teaches that this one God exists in three distinct persons.

Genesis 1:26 "Let *us* make." Here it is shown that there is more than one person in the Godhead.

Genesis 11:7 Here again is an emphasis on there being

more than one person in the Godhead. In this verse, as in 1:26, the persons of the Trinity are in communication with each other.

Isaiah 6:8   Again we see that there is more than one person in the Godhead.

Isaiah 44:6   Two persons of the Godhead are named here: "the Lord the King of Israel" and "his redeemer the Lord of hosts." These are the first and second persons of the Trinity.

Isaiah 48:16   As the previous passage shows that the first and second persons of the Trinity are distinct, so this passage shows that there is another person in the Trinity, the Spirit.

Matthew 3:16, 17   Each of the three persons is shown clearly here. Also read **Matthew 28:19, John 15:26, 1 Peter 1:2.**

Matthew 9:2–7   Jesus Christ claims the power of forgiving sins as his natural right, thus showing that he claims to be God.

Matthew 18:20   Jesus said he was everywhere at once, another claim to deity.

Matthew 28:20   As Jesus is through all space, he is through all time.

John 1:1–3   These verses say that the person called "the Word" is God and made all things. Verses 14 and 15 of this same chapter show that "the Word" is Jesus Christ.

John 5:22   Jesus Christ is to be judge of all mankind. Only God could do this.

John 8:58 Jesus said he was living before the time of Abraham. Abraham lived at 2000 B.C.

John 17:5, 26 Jesus said that he lived with the Father and that the Father loved him before the world was made.

2 Corinthians 5:10 Here again we are told Christ will judge the world.

1 Timothy 3:16 It was Christ who came in the flesh, and here he is called God.

Titus 2:13 Here Jesus is definitely called God.

Thus, the second person of the Trinity is not only distinct from the first person, but he is equally God.

Luke 12:10, 12 Let us now think about the third person of the Trinity. These two verses show that he is God and just as much a person as the first and second persons of the Godhead.

John 15:26 The Spirit is again said to do something only a person can do.

John 16:7–14 The Spirit, or Comforter, is distinct from the second person and does things only a person can do. The Spirit is "he," not "it."

Acts 8:29 Only a person can speak.

Acts 13:2; 15:28; 16:6, 7 The Holy Spirit is a person.

Ephesians 4:30 The above passages show that the Holy Spirit thinks and acts; this verse shows he also feels.

2 Peter 1:21 He is the person of the Trinity who gave us the Bible.

It is central and important to our Christian faith to have clearly in mind the facts concerning the Trinity.

Genesis 1:26; John 17:24 Communication and love existed between the persons of the Trinity before the creation.

2 Corinthians 13:14 The work of each of the three persons is important to us. Jesus died to save us, the Father draws us to himself and loves us, and the Holy Spirit deals with us.

Revelation 1:17, 18 It is because Jesus is God that we can be sure that, after we take him as our Savior, we will have a conscious continuity into the future, go to heaven. He is Alpha and Omega, the first and the last. He is God.

Romans 8:11, 14, 26, 27 The Holy Spirit is a person, and he indwells and leads the Christian and prays for him when the Christian does not know what to pray for himself.

2 / CREATION

In our last study, we saw that the Bible sets forth God as one God but in three persons. We are not worshiping the Christian God unless we worship this God, who is one but three persons.

Likewise, a person is not worshiping the Christian God as he should unless he recognizes that God is sovereign.

When we speak of God's sovereignty, two thoughts are in mind — his work of creation and his work of providence. When we speak of providence, we mean his dealings in the world now.

The following Bible study deals with the Bible's teaching on creation.

Ephesians 1:11; Revelation 4:11   God created all things of his own free will. He did not have to create. Before creation the triune God stood complete, and there was love and communication between the persons of the Trinity. The literal Greek in Revelation 4:11 reads: "Thou art worthy, our Lord, to receive the glory and the honor and the power: for thou did create all things, and because of thy will they existed and were created." He created because he willed to.

Colossians 1:16, 17   Before God created, he dwelt alone.

Psalm 33:9   God created out of nothing. He created by fiat: he spoke and it was.

Genesis 1:1   God created matter. The word "create" used here means to create out of nothing. God created matter out of nothing. He did not just shape pre-existent matter, but brought it into being. He did not make only the world, but the heavens and the earth — everything there is.

Nehemiah 9:6   This verse speaks of God's creation of the "hosts." The text shows that this refers to the angelic hosts. This and other passages teach that God not only created the material universe but angels and souls of men as well — he made them just as he created matter. They are not an extension of himself nor a part of himself. He created them.

Genesis 1:31   After God had created all things he pronounced it good. Both matter and spirit were good as they were originally made. They were not only good in man's judgment but in God's absolute judgment.

If God made us, then we have a responsibility to obey him.

II. GOD'S DEALING WITH MAN

3 / GOD AND MAN

With this study we begin considering what the Bible tells us of the relationship between God and man.

Genesis 2:7 In this verse we are told that God formed the body of men out of the dust of the ground. However, man is more than a body.

Genesis 1:26 Man was made in God's image. This is man's glory, and it is this which sets him off from other creatures. What does it mean that man is made in God's image? Well, among other things it certainly means this: man is moral. This means he can make moral choices. Also, man is rational. This means that he can think. It also means that man is creative — we find that men everywhere make works of art. It is also the reason why man loves.

Genesis 1:31 As God made man, man was good, both in body and soul.

Genesis 3:8a Notice the first phrase in this verse. Man is here shown to be in perfect harmony with God, so that man and God could walk together in the cool of the day. Being in harmony with God, man was also in full harmony with his wife, with nature, and with himself. There was no place for divided personality or schizophrenia in man as he was orginally made. He had power to love and obey God, but as a free agent he could also transgress.

Genesis 2:16, 17 Here stand two parties — God and man. In this verse God states the condition, in order for man to continue in fellowship with God. The condition is simple. Man must show his love for God by obeying him. If man disobeys God, death would be the result. This is more than physical death. Spiritual death, or separation from God, came immediately. Physical death means that which we usually speak of as "death." Eternal death comes at the Judgment. As man was faced with the choice of obedience or disobedience, he had these gracious provisions from God:

a) He was made in the image of God (Genesis 1:26).
b) He had constant fellowship with God (Genesis 3:8a).
c) He was surrounded by a perfect environment (Genesis 2:8).
d) He had a truly free choice, with power to obey or power to transgress. He was not a deterministically conditioned being. He was not programmed (Genesis 2:16, 17).
e) The test was most simple, with both the command and penalty clearly stated (Genesis 2:16, 17).

Genesis 3:1–20 Adam and Eve willfully chose to disobey God.

Genesis 3:7 By trying to cover themselves with the work of their own hands, they showed that guilt had come upon them.

Genesis 3:24 They lost communion with God and were put out of the Garden. Both the body and soul felt the effects of sin.

Genesis 3:17, 18 The external universe is now abnormal. It is not as God made it. It was changed because of man's sin. All that was under man's dominion was affected.

Romans 5:12, 17 Since Adam's fall, all men are sinners. Each time we look upon the body of one who has died, it should remind us that man is a sinner.

Isaiah 53:6

Jeremiah 17:9

Romans 3:10–12, 23

Galatians 3:10

The following two verses point out to us that those who are now Christians were "children of wrath" before they accepted Christ as their Savior.

Ephesians 2:2, 3

Colossians 1:21

It would be well to close our consideration with the fact that each of us personally has sinned in God's sight (1 John 1:10).

In conclusion, God made man. Man's body and soul were good. Man had a true, unprogrammed choice by which he could show his love for God by obedience. Man had continued fellowship with God. He was in a perfect environment. He was given a simple test so that he could demonstrate his love and obedience. Adam and Eve sinned. Since then all men, you and I, have personally sinned.

John 3:18, 36 Having sinned, we are under the judgment of God, under his condemnation, *now*.

4 / GOD'S GRACE (A)

Romans 6:23 Every one of us has earned only one thing at the hand of God, and that is judgment. As far as God's holiness and justice are concerned, he owes us nothing but judgment. He has made us and we have sinned. But the last part of this verse tells us that in spite of this, because of his love, God has provided us with a way of approach to him. It is not because God owes it to us; it is a gift based on his love. Adam and Eve were given a way of work which could please God. However, they sinned and we also have all sinned, and thus this new approach which God gives us cannot be on the basis of our work but of God's grace.

John 3:15, 16 Here we have the triune God standing with his arms open, telling us that even though we are sinners he has provided a way through which "whosoever will" may come.

Philippians 2:7, 8 How can the holy God say "whosoever" to sinners? God cannot just overlook our sin, because he is holy. If he did that, no moral absolute would exist. We can come to God through grace, because Christ worked for us. This finished work is his death upon the cross.

Romans 3:24–26 Because Christ died in substitution, God remains righteous, there is a moral absolute, and yet we do not need to come under his judgment.

John 3:15; 17:4 It is a gift to us, but only on the basis of Christ's perfect work.

1 Peter 1:18, 19 We are purchased with an infinite price.

John 6:29 Christ had to work for us, in his death. But because of his perfect work, we now can approach God simply, by faith, without works.

John 3:15, 16 God's promise is clear. If we accept Jesus as our Savior, then on the basis of Christ's finished work (which we accept by faith alone), we have God's promise of an eternal life. Faith is the empty hand which accepts the gift.

John 3:18, 36 God's penalty is also clear. Because we are sinners, we are already under the condemnation and judgment of God. If we refuse God's gift, if we do not accept Christ's work for us, we remain under the condemnation and judgment of God.

Hebrews 2:3 Adam was commanded to obey God and he sinned. We have all sinned. Therefore, we have earned spiritual, physical, and eternal death. Now God in his love has given us another opportunity. This is not of works, but of grace, in which we partake if we accept his gift. If we accept Christ as our Savior and trust him only for our salvation, if we believe on him and accept his death for us, then we have eternal life. If we refuse God's gracious provision, we stay where we are, under the condemnation and judgment of God.

5 / GOD'S GRACE (B)

Genesis 3:15, 21 As soon as man sinned, God gave the

promise of the coming Savior. He did this in words in verse 15 and by illustration in verse 21. After man sinned, he tried to cover himself with the works of his own hands (verse 7). God took this away and provided a covering of skins. To do this an animal had to be slain. This was an immediate picture that the way man could come to God, now that he had sinned, was not by the humanistic works of his own righteousness but by that which God would provide through the death of the coming Messiah.

Genesis 4:3–5 It would seem that God told Adam and Eve how he wanted them to worship in the future, through the presentation of a lamb as a picture of the coming Messiah. Abel did this, but Cain tried to come on the basis of his own works. Hebrews 11:4 tells us that Abel believed God; Cain did not.

Genesis 12:1–3 The promise which was given to Abraham, 2000 years before Christ came, was twofold — national but also personal. The national promises were and are to the Jews. The spiritual promises were and are to all who would believe God and thus be in the right relationship to the coming Messiah. This Messiah would be one of Abraham's descendants, humanly speaking.

Genesis 22:1–18 Here we have a clear picture in space-time history of the coming Messiah and his substitutionary work. The Old Testament saints had a much clearer concept of Christ's work than we usually attribute to them. Verse 14 ties the events of this chapter at 2000 B.C. into the coming death of Christ 2000 years later. This geographical location was later the geographical location of Jerusalem, where Jesus died. Compare verse 2 with 2 Chronicles 3:1.

Exodus 20:24 Immediately after the Ten Commandments were given, God, in anticipation of man's inability to keep them, provided a way of approach to him. This building of an altar without man's work on it looked forward to the promise of the Messiah, whose work would have none of man's work added to it. No man has ever kept the Ten Commandments perfectly.

Isaiah 53 Now, 700 years before Christ, we see again that the Jews were informed explicitly concerning the work of the coming Messiah. Incidentally, the whole sacrificial system of the Old Testament was a preview of the work of the coming Messiah. The Messiah would come and die for us.

Luke 2:25–32, 36–38 When Jesus was brought to the temple as a baby, Simeon recognized him for who he was: the Messiah prophesied in the Old Testament. There was a remnant in that day who had their personal faith fixed in the coming Messiah. Notice that Anna not only accepted Jesus as the Messiah, for whom she had been looking throughout her life, but she immediately went to tell others in Jerusalem who also had their personal faith fixed in the coming Messiah.

Romans 4:1–3 This states that Abraham, 2000 years before Christ, was saved exactly as we are saved — through faith, without works.

Romans 4:6–8 David (1000 years before Christ) was saved by faith, just as we are saved. The Ten Commandments had been given through Moses 500 years before

David's time. Yet David is clearly said to have been saved not of works, but by faith. No man has ever been saved by his own humanistic works.

Romans 4:10, 11 After Abraham was saved by faith, he was later circumcised. Circumcision did not save him. It was merely an external sign of the fact that he had already been accepted by God through faith alone. No religious good works on our part can help us before the perfect God.

Romans 4:20, 22–25 Abraham was accepted by God because of faith, his believing what God had promised. The same is true of us.

Galatians 3:13, 14 When we receive Christ as our Savior by faith, we receive the same blessing of God Abraham received by faith.

Galatians 3:24 If all this is true, what good then is the law of God, the Ten Commandments, and the other eternal commandments given by God in the Old and New Testaments? The law is meant by God to show us that we are sinners, so that we see our need of accepting Christ as Savior.

Hebrews 11:1–12:2 A long list is given of some of those who in Old Testament times had faith in God. We who have these to look back upon are told also to have the same faith in God, through the acceptance of Christ as our Savior.

Thus through all the ages, before Christ and after Christ alike, there is one way of salvation. All men have sinned. Salvation is available only through faith on the basis of Christ the Messiah's finished work for us.

6 / OLD TESTAMENT PROPHECIES OF THE COMING MESSIAH

After Christ was raised from the dead, he met a number of disciples on the road to Emmaus, but they did not recognize him. We are told that before he made himself known to them, he talked to them, and this is what the Bible says about it:

"And beginning at Moses and all the prophets, he expounded unto them in all the scriptures the things concerning himself" (Luke 24:47).

In other words, on the way to Emmaus he went back into the Old Testament and told them many things that the Old Testament had said concerning him, which he had fulfilled in his life, death, and resurrection. The following are some of the Old Testament passages that foretold the coming of the Messiah. The word "Messiah" in Hebrew is the same as the word "Christ" in Greek, and so one is merely the Old Testament word and the other the New.

The following does not exhaust these Old Testament references. They are only a cross section.

Genesis 3:15 Man has just sinned. God made man perfect and gave him opportunity to obey God and show his love for him. Instead of that, man disobeyed. God then gave a promise to mankind that a Messiah would come, one who would win the victory. This Messiah would come "born of a woman."

Genesis 9:26 Time has passed. We are now in the days of Noah. Now the promise which in Genesis 3:15 was given to the whole human race is narrowed down to one portion of the human race — the Semitic peoples. The

Semitic people today include such races as the Assyrians, Babylonians, Egyptians, Hebrews, Arabians, and a number of others.

Genesis 12:3 More time has passed again. Now, of all the Semitic people, the promise of the coming Messiah is given to one man, Abraham. The coming Savior would be born from his family, i.e. of the Jews.

Genesis 49:10 After Abraham there came Isaac, then Jacob, who had twelve sons. In this passage we are told from which of these twelve families the Messiah would come. He would be born of the tribe of Judah.

Exodus 12:46 We now enter another phase of the picture which is being drawn of the coming Messiah. This was written about 1500 years before Christ. The passages given above occurred even before that time. Here Moses is saying that in regard to the passover lamb, which prefigured the coming of the Messiah, that none of its bones should be broken. Notice how carefully John 19:36 points out that no bones of Christ were broken, even though he was crucified and even though this was not the case with the two thieves who were crucified with him.

Deuteronomy 18:15 We are still about 1500 years before Christ. Moses here gives a different line again concerning the coming one. We are told here something of his work. When he comes, he will be an unusual and unique prophet. A prophet according to Scripture is not basically one who tells the future but rather one who speaks for God to men.

2 Samuel 7:16 The line is now narrowed down again. Of all the tribe of Judah, the Christ must come from a certain family. That family is the royal family of David. See Matthew 1:1 and 22:42.

Psalm 2:2 The picture of the coming Christ has grown more clear — what he must be, how he must act, what he must do if he is to be really the Messiah, the Savior of the world. In verse 7 we are told that this one is to be more than a man; God calls him his Son. See Acts 13:33, Hebrews 1:5. The 12th verse urges each to come into the right personal relationship with this Messiah.

Psalm 16:8–11 Here we are told another thing about the Messiah. He will die but his body will not remain in the grave. He will be raised from the dead. See Acts 2:25–31.

Psalm 22:1–18 This is a tremendous picture of the crucifixion of Christ. The Jews did not crucify; they stoned to death. The only nation that would crucify as a general practice would be the Romans. This passage in the book of Psalms was written about 1000 years before Jesus lived and died. Yet the picture given here of Jesus' death is a perfect picture of crucifixion. Notice too the many details fulfilled at Christ's death.

Psalm 41:9 When this Messiah would come, he would be betrayed by one who had been close to him. Jesus was so betrayed, of course, by Judas. See John 13:18, Acts 1:16.

Psalm 69:9 This is quoted of Jesus when he cleansed the temple of those who had turned it into a place of commerce. See John 2:17.

Psalm 69:21 When Jesus was dying, this is exactly what happened to him. See Matthew 27:34.

Psalm 110:1–4 Moses, 500 years before this psalm was written, said that the Messiah would be a prophet. This passage tells us he would also be a priest. A priest is very different from a prophet. A prophet speaks for God to men; a priest represents men before God. See Acts 2: 32–34.

Isaiah 7:14 Here we have a stupendous sign. When the Messiah came, he would have a human mother but no human father. See Matthew 1:23.

Isaiah 9:6, 7 Notice the names given to the coming Messiah. Obviously he is to be more than a man; he is also to be God.

Isaiah 42:1–3, 6, 7 We have already seen that this Messiah would be born of a woman, without a human father, and would be God. But he would also be a servant, and this servant would open the way of blessing for Jews and Gentiles as well. See Matthew 12:17–21, Luke 2:32.

Isaiah 50:6 Here we are told something of the things that Jesus would suffer. The New Testament says this is exactly what happened to him. They hit him. They beat him. They did everything, not only to hurt, but to humiliate him. See Matthew 26:67; 27:26.

Isaiah 52:13 to the end of Isaiah 53 This one was to be a priest in a very special way. He was to be a priest by himself bearing our sins. He was to be a suffering Messiah, to die for us.

Jeremiah 31:15 The New Testament says this was fulfilled literally when the little children were killed by King Herod at the time of Jesus' birth, in Herod's attempt to kill the coming Messiah who the wise men said had been born. See Matthew 2:17, 18.

Micah 5:2 Here we are told the exact city where the Messiah would have to be born: the town of Bethlehem. This verse also says that he has existed from the days of eternity. See Matthew 2:6.

Zechariah 9:9 Now we come to the third part of the work of Christ. Moses said he would be a prophet. Psalms and Isaiah designated him as a priest. Zechariah clearly says he is to be a king. Jesus literally fulfilled this passage when he came in triumphal entry into Jerusalem just before his death. See Matthew 21:5.

Zechariah 11:11–13 We are told here exactly how much Judas would receive for betraying Christ. See Matthew 26:15.

Jesus fulfilled each of these literally. The possibility of any one man having done all these things, let alone being all that was designated, was impossible as a matter of coincidence. Jesus fulfilled them all because he is what the Bible said he would be. He is God, and man born of a virgin, the one promised for thousands of years. When he came, all these things came to pass. These, then, are just a few of the things that Jesus must have talked about with the disciples on the road to Emmaus.

7 / CHRIST THE MEDIATOR — HIS PERSON

1 Timothy 2:5 Notice that this verse says there is only one mediator between God and man. That one mediator is the man Christ Jesus. There are not several possible mediators; Jesus Christ is the *only* one. He is the only possible intercessor between God the Father and man.

I. *The Person of Christ the Mediator*

a) First of all, let's review some of our observations in the previous study, "The God of the Bible." You will remember that in this we saw that the Bible clearly teaches that Jesus Christ is truly God, equally God as is God the Father. We saw that the second person of the Trinity was God before he was born to Mary; he was God while he was on the earth; and he is God now. We also saw that the second person of the Trinity is distinct from the first person of the Trinity, the Father, and from the third person of the Trinity, the Holy Spirit. The second person of the Trinity is God the Son. In the conclusion of that study we said, "It is because Jesus is God that we can be sure that, after we take him as our Savior, we will have a conscious continuity into the future, go to heaven. He is Alpha and Omega, the first and the last."

b) The Bible also teaches that Jesus Christ is truly man. In our day most heresies deny the true deity of Christ, but in the early church the common heresy was the denial of the true humanity of Christ. We should remember that from God's viewpoint, it is far more wonderful that the second person of the Trinity became a man than that he is God. He had been God for eternity — he became a man when he was born.

Matthew 4:2 Christ became hungry.

Matthew 8:24 He slept.

Matthew 26:38 Jesus Christ had a soul as well as a body. See also 1 Peter 3:18, 19.

Luke 1:32 On his human side, Christ descended from a human family.

Luke 2:40, 52 He grew physically and mentally.

Luke 22:44 Christ suffered anguish.

Luke 23:46 He died.

Luke 24:39 After his resurrection, he still had a true body.

John 11:33, 35 Jesus wept.

John 19:28 Christ suffered thirst.

John 19:34 He had blood in his veins.

Romans 5:15 Adam was a man, and Christ was a man.

Galatians 4:4 This verse tells us that God the Father sent forth his Son, and after that he, the Son, was also a man.

1 Timothy 3:16 This verse tells us specifically that God revealed himself in the flesh, that is, as a man.

When men looked at Jesus Christ, they saw only one person, but he had two natures. He is truly God and truly man.

Hebrews 2:14, 18 God became man in order to become our mediator.

Hebrews 4:15 Our mediator knows how we feel, even in our temptations, because he is man as well as God.

Hebrews 13:8 Having become a man, he will always be man and God.

1 John 4:1, 2 The Bible says that it is most important to believe that Jesus has always been God and that at a point of history he became a man. In this verse, we are told that it is upon this point that we are to test religious teachers, spirits, and systems. If they do not teach that Jesus has always been God and that he became truly a man, they are not Christian.

   c) How did the unique Son of God become a man?

Isaiah 7:14 Seven hundred years before Jesus was born, it was prophesied that he would be born of a virgin. See Matthew 1:23.

Galatians 4:4 Notice that Paul says that Christ was born of a woman. No father is mentioned, and this would have been against Jewish usage if he had had a father.

Genesis 3:15 In this first promise of the coming Savior, the seed of the woman is mentioned. No father is mentioned.

Luke 1:27–38 It is interesting that Luke was a doctor, and that he gives the most detail about the virgin birth of Christ.

Matthew 1:18–25 Joseph had the most to lose if Jesus was not virgin born. But he was convinced that Mary had not been unfaithful, that the child to be born to Mary would have no human father, and that God alone was its father. The fact that Joseph was convinced after his original suspicion of Mary is strong testimony of the virgin birth.

Thus, concerning the person of Christ the mediator — he has always been God. Ever since he was born to Mary in the virgin birth, the incarnation, he has been one person with two natures. He is truly God and truly man forever.

This is the one who is our mediator. There is no other.

8 / CHRIST THE MEDIATOR — HIS WORK: PROPHET

II. *The Work of Christ the Mediator*

When we think of the work of Christ as mediator, we usually think of his death. This is especially true in our day because many people who have departed from the teaching of the Bible put all their emphasis on the moral facets of Christianity. Therefore, we in reaction are apt to speak only of the death of Christ. However, the Bible teaches us that there are three parts to Christ's work.

A. As we have already seen, Christ is a prophet. A prophet is one who reveals the things of God to men. It is the giving of true knowledge, propositional knowledge.

Luke 13:33   Christ here says that he is a prophet.

Deuteronomy 18:15, 18   The Old Testament said the coming Messiah would be a prophet. Compare this passage with Acts 3:22, 23, which states that Christ fulfilled this.

John 1:18   However, Christ is not just *a* prophet. He is a *unique* prophet. He is the person of the Godhead who reveals the triune God to man.

John 1:1, 2   Here Christ is called the Word (see verses 14, 15). This signifies the fact that he is the one who reveals God to men. Vv. 14 and 15 make clear that "the Word" is Jesus Christ.

1 Corinthians 10:1–4   This passage indicates that it was Christ, the second person of the Trinity, who was the revealer of the things of God to the Old Testament people of God.

1 Peter 1:10, 11   This reaffirms this.

Colossians 2:9 While on the earth, Christ revealed the triune God to men. By considering Christ, we can learn about the character of God. Christ taught men facts concerning the past, present, and future by his spoken words.

1 John 5:20 Christ came in the incarnation to give us true knowledge.

John 14:26; 16:12–14 Here Christ promises that after his death, resurrection, and ascension he will still continue to give knowledge to men through the Holy Spirit who will be coming. This is especially a promise that he will teach us the things of God in the New Testament.

9 / CHRIST THE MEDIATOR – HIS WORK: PRIEST

B. Since man has fallen into sin, he needs more than knowledge. He also needs holiness and righteousness. Thus, Christ not only acts as a prophet, in giving us knowledge, but also acts as a priest. As priest, he removes the guilt of sin from us and provides for us true holiness and righteousness.

Psalm 110:4; Zechariah 6:13 These Old Testament prophecies predicted that when the Messiah came, he would do a priestly work.

Mark 10:45 Christ came to die. This was his great priestly work.

John 1:29 John called Christ the Lamb of God, thus signifying that Christ would die to take away the guilt which is ours because of sin. By the term "Lamb of God," John also showed that the Old Testament sacrificial system was a type or illustration of the work Christ would do for us in a complete and final way by his death. That death was the act which the Old Testament sacrifices had fore-shadowed.

1 Corinthians 5:7 Christ is here called our passover, and he died for us. The passover lamb of Exodus 12 was a type or illustration of the work which Christ would do for those who believe on him.

Ephesians 5:2 This verse says specifically that Christ gave himself in his death as an offering and a sacrifice.

Hebrews 3:1 The book of Hebrews gives more detail on the priestly work of Christ than any other biblical writing. This verse says Christ is our High Priest.

Hebrews 4:14; 6:20 Christ is our High Priest not only when he was on earth, but now and forever.

Hebrews 5:5, 6 As a priest, Christ fulfilled the prophecy of Psalm 110:4.

Hebrews 7:26, 27 Christ's high-priestly work is different in three ways from that of the Old Testament priests:

1. He is perfectly sinless.

2. He made a sacrifice that will never need to be repeated.

3. The sacrifice he offered was himself.

Hebrews 8:1 Since his ascension, Christ our High Priest is on the right hand of God the Father.

Hebrews 9:11–15 Again the Scriptures emphasize that the sacrifice was Christ himself, and that when the sacrifice was once made, it never needed to be repeated. Being God, Christ's sacrifice, his death, had infinite value.

Hebrews 9:25–28 Again it is emphasized that Christ's sacrifice was once for all. Just as men die only once, just as certainly there cannot be (and does not need to be) any repetition of Christ's sacrifice.

Hebrews 10:11–14   The sacrifice was once for all. Because of who Christ the High Priest is, a single offering, his once-for-all death for us is enough.

Hebrews 10:19–22   Once we have accepted Christ as our Savior, we can have confidence in the presence of the holy God.

1 Peter 3:18   In the Greek the word translated "once" means "once for all." So Peter is saying that Christ's sacrifice cannot, and need not, be repeated. From this and preceding verses we have considered, it is clear that Christ as our priest gave himself as the sacrifice upon Calvary's cross at a point of space-time history, so that he might once for all bear the punishment which we deserve because of the guilt of our sin.

1 John 4:10   Christ's work is substitutionary, the expiation for our sins. In other words, he took the punishment rightly due to us because of our sin.

1 John 2:1   After we accept Christ as our Savior, we should strive not to sin. But if we sin, Christ is on the right hand of God the Father as our advocate. Christ's sacrifice on the cross was complete; but he now continues his high-priestly work by interceding for us in heaven. Remember Hebrews 4:14, 6:20.

Hebrews 9:24   Christ is in heaven, in the presence of the Father, for us.

Hebrews 7:25   Christ's sacrifice being perfect, he continues his priestly work and is able to save us completely and forever.

John 17:9 This is the high-priestly prayer of Christ which he prayed shortly before his death. In this verse we see that Christ does not intercede for everyone. He prays for those who, by God's grace, have accepted him as their Savior.

John 17:20 Christ interceded at that time, and does so now in heaven. He intercedes for all who have believed on him on the basis of the testimony of those who were firsthand witnesses. This testimony is given in the New Testament in connection with the Old.

Romans 8:34 Once we have accepted Christ as our Savior, neither Satan nor man can successfully condemn us, because Christ died for us and now intercedes for us.

Christ's intercession in heaven is based upon the substitutionary atonement which he wrought for us when he died upon the cross. His intercession for us can never fail, because in his death he merits all he asks on our behalf. Christ is our priest; we need no other.

10 / CHRIST THE MEDIATOR — HIS WORK: KING

C. Christ is also king.

Genesis 49:10 Here we have the first promise that the coming Messiah will be a king.

2 Samuel 7:16 (with Matthew 1:1, 22:42) Here the Lord tells David that the coming Messiah will come from among his descendants. Thus the Messiah will be of the kingly line.

Psalm 2:6 Again we see the Messiah as king.

Isaiah 9:6, 7 We usually use this as one of the Christmas verses. But notice that it says specifically that the Messiah will be of the line of David; he will be a king.

Micah 5:2 This verse reaffirms the same point, that the Messiah will be a ruler.

Zechariah 6:13 This verse unites two thoughts. The coming Messiah will be a priest and a king.

Luke 1:31–33 The angel makes the promise to Mary that the child which will be born to her will be a Savior (his name will be "Jesus"). He will be God, and on his human side he will be of the family of David. He will be a king.

Matthew 2:2 When the wise men came, they were looking for the King of the Jews. Verse 6 connects this with Micah 5:2.

John 1:49 Nathanael realized that Christ was the Messiah, the King of the Jews.

Luke 19:37, 38 On Palm Sunday, the Sunday before Christ's crucifixion, for one short moment Jesus was proclaimed as king. Verse 40 shows that Christ accepted this.

John 18:37 Christ here acknowledges before Pilate that he is king.

John 19:2, 3, 12, 14, 15, 19, 21, 22 When the people were mocking Jesus, they did it in such a way that they made fun of his kingship. Verse 12 seems to indicate that if he had rejected this claim, the case against him would have collapsed.

Acts 17:7 After his death and resurrection, Jesus' followers still taught that Jesus was king.

Christ is king in three ways:

1. Christ is head over all things now.

Matthew 28:18 Right now all power is given to Christ in heaven and earth.

Ephesians 1:20–22 Today Christ, on the right hand of God the Father, is head over all things for the church.

2. The second coming of Christ.

Hebrews 2:8 There will come a time when Christ will rule in a way that he does not rule now. See also 1 Corinthians 15:24, 25.

Acts 1:6, 7 Just before Christ's ascension, he was asked when he would establish his kingdom upon the earth. He did not say he never would do so, but that the time was not yet come.

1 Timothy 6:14, 15 When Christ comes back again, he will then be King of kings and Lord of lords in a new way.

Matthew 25:31–34 When Christ returns, he will judge as king.

Revelation 17:14; 19:16 Again we see Christ, when he returns as King of kings and Lord of lords. The Bible tells us that at that time every knee shall bow before him (Philippians 2:10, 11). This does not necessarily mean that every knee will wish to bow before him but will bow of necessity, even if the individual sinful heart is still in rebellion against him.

3. Christ, the king of our lives.

Colossians 1:13 When we have accepted Christ as our Savior, we have stepped from the power of darkness into the kingdom of Christ. Thus, we who have received Christ are in his kingdom now.

Ephesians 5:23, 24 Christ is now head of the Church, which is made up of all who have accepted him as Savior. Once we have done this, we are to obey him.

Luke 19:11–27 In this whole passage, Christ teaches us that after we have accepted him as our Savior, we, as now his servants, are responsible for serving him and will be held accountable for the way we do serve him. If we serve him well, he will then say to us, "Well done, thou good and faithful servant." Verses 14 and 27 contrast the servants with the citizens, who should serve him as God and Creator but are still in rebellion.

When we have taken Jesus as our Savior, he should be the king and Lord of our lives now.

The story is told that when Queen Victoria was a young girl, she was present at a concert where Handel's "Messiah" was played. Everyone stood when the music rang out, "King of kings, Lord of lords." When Victoria also rose, others who were with her restrained her, saying she should not stand because she was queen. Victoria answered, "I am Queen of England, but Christ is my King of kings and Lord of lords." After we have accepted Christ as our Savior, then indeed he should in reality be our king, just as he is our prophet and priest.

11 / CHRIST'S HUMILIATION AND EXALTATION

When we consider Christ's work as a whole, we find that it presents two aspects: his humiliation and his exaltation.

1. *Christ's Humiliation*

John 17:5 Here Christ speaks of the glory which he had had with God from before the creation of the world.

Philippians 2:6, 7 When Christ came into the world through the virgin birth, he humbled himself so that the Creator of all the universe became the servant.

John 1:14 The Creator (verse 3) took upon himself the form of a man. He "became flesh."

Luke 2:7 When Christ was born, he was not born of a great human family, but to a very poor one. When he was born, there was not even a home to shelter him or a room in the public inn, but he was born in a stable.

John 7:52 Christ did not even come from a respected portion of the country, but from Galilee, which was looked down upon by the Jews.

Mark 6:3 His family was not one of the great ones of the community. Joseph, the husband of Mary, was a carpenter, and Jesus followed his trade.

Galatians 4:4 The great Lawgiver placed himself under the law.

Philippians 2:8 The one who himself deserved obedience from all creation became obedient.

Galatians 3:13 The righteous judge of all the universe placed himself under the curse of the law. He identified himself with sinful mankind.

Matthew 4:1–11; Hebrews 4:15 The Holy One allowed himself to suffer every temptation that mankind can know. Consider what pain it must have been for him to be daily buffeted by the sin that permeates the world in which we live.

John 1:11 The Jews, who were his ancient people, rejected him.

John 7:3–5 His own half brothers, i.e., the natural children born to Mary and Joseph after Jesus' birth, rejected him until after his death and resurrection.

Matthew 27:46 As he hung upon the cross, having taken upon himself the sin of those who would trust him as Savior, God the Father turned from him. His physical sufferings were great, but not the greatest part of his suffering.

Luke 22:47, 48 Judas, one of his friends, betrayed him with a kiss.

Matthew 26:56 All his disciples forsook him in his hour of need.

Matthew 27:11–50 Consider the various forms of humiliation and agony heaped upon Jesus in these hours. Remember that this is God who allowed himself to be so treated.

2 Corinthians 5:21 The eternally Holy One died as sin for us.

1 Peter 3:18, 19 Like natural man, his spirit and body were unnaturally torn asunder when he died. His body rested in the grave. His soul descended into Hades, the place of departed spirits.

2. *Christ's Exaltation*

Acts 2:25–31 At this point comes a great change. Through Christ's humiliation his steps have been downward all the way. Now comes the increasing glory. First, while his body lay in the grave, it did not see corruption.

Luke 24:36–43 The human body and the human soul of Christ are reunited. It was not just Christ's spirit which rose from the dead. It was the complete man with body and spirit reunited.

John 20:25-28 Christ's resurrected body was the same body which the disciples had known before his death. Thomas' conquered skepticism is one proof of the physical resurrection of Christ, of the fact that the body which came out of the garden tomb was the one that had been placed in it.

Acts 1:3 Jesus, with his resurrection body, was seen from time to time over a forty-day period. This is spoken of here as infallible proof.

Acts 1:9–11 After Jesus had showed himself upon the earth for many days after his resurrection, he was taken up into heaven. He went from one place, earth, to another, heaven. His baptism began his public ministry (Matthew 3:13–17). His ascension showed it to be terminated.

John 14:2, 3 In this place called heaven, Christ is now preparing a place for us.

Acts 2:32, 33 The exaltation of the Lord Jesus Christ continues.

Ephesians 1:20–22 The one who was spat upon and

humiliated before the eyes of sinful men is now head over all things.

Revelation 19:9–16 When Christ comes back again to the earth, Gentile and Jew alike will know that the one they humiliated and crucified is what he claimed to be: the Old Testament-prophesied Messiah, the only Savior of men, King of kings, Lord of lords, and indeed our sovereign God.

III. SALVATION

12 / SALVATION — HOW?

With this study we begin a completely new topic. We've already looked at "God," and "God's Dealing with Man." This third topic is "Salvation," how it is received and what it includes.

How do we obtain salvation? The Bible's answer, as we have already partially seen in our study of God's grace, is that salvation is obtained by faith in Christ, plus nothing.

John 3:15, 16, 18 We have used these verses a number of times, but they are worth looking at again to see how clearly Christ says that salvation is received by faith in him, plus nothing.

John 3:36 John the Baptist emphasizes that salvation is through faith plus nothing.

Romans 3:9–20 By the deeds of the law, that is, by good works, no man is or can be just in the sight of God.

Isaiah 64:6 Even our best works are not good enough in the sight of the Holy God. Even when the outward acts are good, who can completely untangle all the mixed and complex motives which move us?

Galatians 3:24 God never gave the law (the Ten Commandments, the Sermon on the Mount, or any other commands) as though salvation would come through the keeping of it. As far as salvation goes, each of God's laws shows us that we need Christ.

Romans 2:1–3 Men do not even keep their own made-up norms, by which they judge others.

Acts 16:30–33 Just as moral good works cannot save us, so also religious good works cannot save us. Baptism is a sign of salvation, not the basis for it.

Romans 4:9–11 It was the same in the Old Testament. Abraham put his faith in God. The circumcision came later. Religious good works cannot save.

Romans 9:6 Not all the Old Testament Jews were true spiritual Israel. Neither today will church membership in itself save. Salvation is indeed ours only on the basis of faith in Christ, plus nothing.

Galatians 2:16 Salvation is never on the basis of any kind of good works.

Romans 3:21–26 Good works cannot save us, but faith in Christ will. The word "freely" in verse 24 means "gratis." There is no cost to us.

John 8:24 There is only one way of salvation. If we do not accept Christ as our Savior, we remain under the judgment of God.

John 14:6 There are not many ways of salvation. There is only one way to come to God the Father.

Acts 4:12 It is faith in Christ or nothing.

As you finish looking up these verses, I urge you to consider Christ's invitation: "Him that comes to me I will not cast out" (John 6:37). *The basis* is the finished, substitutionary death of Christ. *The instrument* by which we accept the free gift is faith. Faith has a double significance: it is believing God's promises, and it is the empty hand which accepts the gift without trying to add humanistic religious or moral good works to it.

13 / JUSTIFICATION

Romans 1:16 As the word "salvation" is used here and throughout the New Testament, it has a much wider meaning than is usually given to it today. Today it is often limited to becoming a Christian. The scriptural use of the term includes all those things in the past, present, and future which will come to the man or woman who has accepted Christ as his or her Savior. In this lesson, we will consider the first of these things.

1. Justification

Romans 3:20 We cannot be justified on the basis of our good works.

James 2:10 In order to be justified before God on the basis of our good works, we would have to be perfect, without one sinful act or sinful thought from our birth to our death. The word "gospel" means "good news." Telling a person to be good is not good news. For example, if a person were in jail for some crime and someone rushed up to him and shouted, "Good news!," the person looking through the bars would expect word of possible liberation. If the friend's message were instead, "Be good," it would be foolish and cruel. So it is if we would say,

"Be good" to the man already bound by sin and marked with its guilt.

Luke 15:11–24 The story of the prodigal son teaches us many things. For example, it tells us that our justification is not our being made good. It is not an infused righteousness, not a work wrought within us. When the sinner comes back to God the Father through faith in the Lord Jesus Christ, the Father does not send him first to be cleaned up and then receive him, but immediately puts his arms about him. The arms of the Father are placed about us in that moment when we accept Christ as our Savior, even though we still bear the scars of our sin.

Romans 4:1–9, 22–25 Justification is the declaration on God's part that we are just in his sight because he has imputed to us the obedience of Christ. This means that God charges our sins to Christ's account. He attributes to us the obedience of Christ. It is as if a little child enters a store and buys more than he can pay for. Then the parent arrives and says, "Charge that to my account." The child's debt is erased. The parent pays. When we are justified, God charges the punishment due to the guilt of our sin to the account of Christ.

Romans 5:1 Once we are declared just by God, there is peace between God and us.

Colossians 2:13, 14 It is not that God overlooks our sins. God cannot do this, for he is holy. It is that our sins have actually been punished in the sufferings of Christ upon the cross.

Isaiah 38:17; 43:25; Micah 7:19 When we have been

declared just by God, it is as though God has dropped the guilt of our sins into the deepest sea. The justification is not merely a pardon but, as has been said, once we have been justified, it is "just as though we have never sinned."

Isaiah 53:4, 5, The ground for our justification is the perfect work of Christ on Calvary.

Romans 5:8, 9 This is the wonder of the love of God — that while we were sinners, Christ died for us. Because Christ has died for us (Romans 3:26), God can be just and yet declare our sins forgiven.

Acts 13:38, 39 The instrument by which we lay hold of this great gift of God is faith in Jesus Christ.

Romans 3:28 Justification is by faith, plus nothing.

Galatians 2:16 There is only one way to be justified before the holy God, and that is by faith in Christ.

What is faith in Christ? A missionary when seeking a native word for faith could not find it. Finally, he sat in a chair and raised his feet from the ground, putting his full weight on the chair and bearing none of his weight himself. He then asked what word described his act, and used that word for faith. This is an accurate picture.

Faith in Christ is resting totally on him and his finished work.

14 / THE NEW RELATIONSHIP: ADOPTION

When we accept Christ as our Savior, we are immediately justified. Another aspect of the salvation which is immediately ours is that which we will consider in this study — adoption.

2. *Adoption by God the Father*

John 1:12   When we accept Christ as our Savior, we become the children of God. This indicates that we are not God's children until we do accept Christ. God made us all but we are the children of God only as we come through Jesus Christ.

2 Corinthians 6:18   In most Bible verses men and women together are spoken of as "the sons of God." But here we have a very touching passage where God speaks of the women who come to him through Christ as "his daughters."

Galatians 4:4, 5   Christ is the eternal Son of God. He is unique. He is the only begotten Son. But when we take Christ as our Savior, we receive the adoption of sons. In other words, we are adopted by God the Father as his children.

John 20:17   Christ is very careful to make a clear distinction between his unique and eternal Sonship and our becoming the children of God.

Ephesians 1:3–5   Once we have taken Christ as our Savior and so are God the Father's children, we may come into his presence with all boldness. As the child of a king may come into the king's presence as his child, so we may come into the presence of Almighty God, the Creator. We may rightfully say to him, "Thou art our Father," and he says to us, "Ye are my children."

1 John 3:1   This is the consummation of God's love, that when we accept Christ as our Savior we are the sons of God.

Matthew 6:32   When I am a child of God, he is concerned about my material needs.

Luke 12:32   In the midst of deepest trouble, we can be sure that the Father's hand is upon us for good.

Romans 8:15   When God is our Father, we may call him "Abba," i.e. "Daddy," or "Papa."

Romans 8:17   When God is our Father, we are joint-heirs with Christ. Think what this means. The riches of heaven are ours, not only after death but in this life as well.

Galatians 4:6   As soon as God becomes our Father, these blessings are ours, including the indwelling of the Holy Spirit. We do not have to wait for death for these blessings of salvation.

Hebrews 12:5–11   Once God has become our Father, many blessings are ours, and among them is this: As a human father who deeply loves his child chastens his child when he is naughty, so God our Father brings things into our lives to keep us close to himself. After we have taken Christ as our Savior, and God is our Father, our sins have been all punished on Calvary. But the Father allows hard things to come into our lives when we wander away from him, so our lives may experience "the peaceable fruit of righteousness," which is not only righteousness but peace.

15 / THE NEW RELATIONSHIP: IDENTIFIED AND UNITED WITH GOD THE SON

After we have put our faith in Christ, we are identified and united with Christ.

Romans 8:1 After we have accepted Christ as Savior, we are in Christ.

1 Corinthians 6:17 We are joined to, united with, Christ.

Galatians 2:20 Christ lives in me.

Ephesians 1:3 We are in Christ.

Ephesians 1:6, 7; 2:1–6, 13 These verses all restate this glorious truth — we are in Christ. See also Colossians 2:10.

Christ is the Bridegroom, we are the bride.

Matthew 22:2–14; 25:10 Our union with Christ is like a marriage. Christ is the Bridegroom.

Romans 7:4 When we accept Christ as Savior, we are married to Christ. As natural marriage brings forth children, so our union with Christ should produce fruit for God.

2 Corinthians 11:2 A bride who loves her husband has her mind only on him and is faithful to him. So we should have our minds fixed on Christ.

Ephesians 5:31, 32 Marriage is a picture of the believer's union with Christ.

Revelation 19:7–9 At the second coming of Christ, there will be a great event known as "the marriage supper of the Lamb (Christ)."

Revelation 22:17 The bride, those who have taken Christ as Savior, should be busy inviting others to partake in this high privilege and honor. As a bride talks very naturally about her beloved, so our conversation should be much about Christ.

Christ is the vine, we are the branches.

John 15:1–5 The life of the vine flows into the branches to bring forth fruit. In the same way, those who have accepted Christ as Savior have a vital union with Christ. His life flows into us to bring forth spiritual fruit.

Christ is the Head. The Church (those who have received Christ as Savior) is the body.

Romans 12:5 As the body has many parts, yet is one body, so we who have accepted Christ as Savior are many; yet we are one body, the Church, the body of Christ.

1 Corinthians 12:11–27 As the body's health depends on the condition of all its parts, so it is important for all the Christians to be in good spiritual condition. As the body is subject to the direction of the head, so we should constantly do the bidding of Christ.

Ephesians 1:22, 23; 4:15, 16; 5:30; Colossians 1:18 The Church (all who have accepted Christ as Savior) is Christ's body.

Christ is the Foundation; we are the spiritual house built on it.

1 Peter 2:2–6 We are living stones.

The only begotten Son of God is called our brother, as we become the adopted children of God.

Hebrews 2:16, 17 As the natural son of a household is the brother of the adopted child, so Christ is our wonderful Elder Brother when we take him as our Savior.

In our studies of Christ as mediator we have seen that when we take Christ as our Savior, God the Son is our prophet, priest, and king. Christ is our prophet, and in fellowship with him the believer is a prophet.

John 16:13; 1 John 2:27 Through Christ we have true knowledge, knowledge that we should give to a dying world which is in confusion, intellectually lost in unrelatedness. God has given us the Bible to give us true knowledge.

Christ is our priest, and in fellowship with him every believer is a priest.

1 Peter 2:5, 9; Revelation 1:6, 5:10, 20:6 Every believer has the privilege of coming immediately into the presence of God in prayer. We should diligently avail ourselves of this privilege, including prayer for the non-Christians about us. We should seek to lead those who do not know Christ as Savior to him, the great High Priest.

Romans 12:1, 2 Every believer has the privilege of offering himself to God as a living sacrifice.
Christ is our king, and with him the believer is a king.

1 Peter 2:9; Revelation 1:6; 3:21; 5:10; 20:6 We are a *royal* priesthood. We shall reign with Christ, on the earth when Christ comes back again.

It is by being united with Christ that we can bring forth fruit in all the phases of our lives.

John 15:5 Abiding in Christ is the secret of fruitbearing.

2 Corinthians 12:9 It is not our strength, but the strength of Christ in the midst of our weakness.

Ephesians 2:10; 3:17–19 After becoming united with Christ, we should bring forth good works.

Philippians 1:11   The fruit we should bring forth after we are Christians must be by Christ working in and through us.

Colossians 2:10   We have all we need in Christ, for this life as well as for eternity.

16 / THE NEW RELATIONSHIP: GOD THE HOLY SPIRIT INDWELLS THE CHRISTIAN

The third aspect of the new relationship, which is immediately ours when we accept Christ as Savior, is that God the Holy Spirit dwells within us.

Joel 2:28, 29   The Old Testament prophesied this.

John 14:16, 17; 7:38, 39; 16:7; Acts 1:5   Christ promised this.

Matthew 3:11   John the Baptist so spoke concerning Christ.

Acts 2:1–18   The promise and prophecy were fulfilled after Christ had died, had risen, and had ascended into heaven.

Acts 2:38; 1 John 4:13   All Christians are immediately indwelt by the Holy Spirit when they accept Christ as Savior.

Romans 8:9   There is no such thing as a person who has accepted Christ as Savior who is not at once indwelt by the Holy Spirit.

1 Corinthians 3:16   The Holy Spirit dwells in all who have received Christ.

1 Corinthians 6:19   The body of the believer is the temple of the Holy Spirit. The temple in Jerusalem was destroyed a few years after this was written. Believers' bodies are now God's temple.

2 Timothy 1:14   The Holy Spirit lives in the Christian.

Here are some examples of the Holy Spirit's activity:

John 16:8   The Spirit reproves the world of sin. Because the Christian is indwelt by the Holy Spirit, his life should reprove the world of sin.

John 3:5, 6,   Regeneration is the Spirit's work.

John 15:26; 16:14; Acts 5:32   He bears witness to Christ.

1 Corinthians 12:4, 13; Ephesians 2:22   He builds the Church (those who are real Christians) into a well-balanced whole.

2 Corinthians 13:14   The indwelling Spirit deals with the Christian. He communicates to the believer the benefits of redemption.

John 14:16–18; Romans 8:9–11   When the Holy Spirit dwells in us, Christ dwells in us.

John 14:23   When the Holy Spirit dwells in us, both the Father and the Son abide, make their home, with us. The indwelling Holy Spirit is the agent of the whole Trinity as he indwells us.

John 14:26; 15:26; 16:7; Acts 9:31   The indwelling Holy Spirit is the Christian's Comforter. The Greek word translated "Comforter" is a hard word to translate. It can also be counselor, advocate, protector, supporter. It means "one called to one's side to help."

John 14:26; 16:13; 1 Corinthians 2:12, 13; Hebrews 10: 15, 16; 1 John 2:20, 27   The indwelling Spirit is our teacher, especially in opening our minds to understand the Bible.

Acts 1:8 He is the Christian's source of power.

Luke 12:11, 12 He gives the believer the right words in time of persecution.

Romans 5:5; 14:7; 15:13; 1 Thessalonians 1:6; Galatians 5:22, 23 The indwelling Spirit gives the Christian graces of love, joy, peace, hope, longsuffering, etc. As *all* Christians are indwelt by the Spirit, the fruit of the Spirit is to have meaning for *all* Christians.

"The great distinction of a true Christian is the indwelling of the Holy Spirit. How careful should he be, lest anything in his thoughts or feelings would be offensive to this divine guest!" — Dr. Charles Hodge

This new relationship with the triune God is, then, the second of the blessings of salvation, justification being the first. This new relationship is threefold:

1. God the Father is the Christian's Father.

2. The only begotten Son of God is our Savior and Lord, our prophet, priest, and king. We are identified and united with him.

3. The Holy Spirit lives in us and deals with us. He communicates to us the manifold benefits of redemption.

17 / THE NEW RELATIONSHIP: THE BROTHERHOOD OF BELIEVERS

We have seen that when we take Christ as Savior we are immediately justified, and we immediately have a new relationship with God the Father, God the Son, and God the Holy Spirit.

When we come into this new relationship with the triune God, all those who have ever trusted Christ as their Savior are our brothers and sisters. This has been usually spoken of as "the communion of saints."

Matthew 23:8 Not all men are brothers, according to the biblical use of that word. We are all created by God. As all are descendants of Adam and Eve, all men are "my kind" and are to be carefully treated as neighbors (Luke 10:27–37). But in the terms of the Bible, we are brothers to those who have Christ as their Savior and therefore have God as their father.

Galatians 6:10 We are to do good to *all* men, but there is a clear line between "the household of faith" and others.

Ephesians 2:19 Before we took Christ as our Savior, we were strangers and foreigners. But when we became Christians we were made fellow citizens with all others who had done the same.

1 Thessalonians 5:14, 15 Again we are told to do good to all men, but especially to our brethren in the faith.

1 Peter 2:17 We have a special relationship to those who are brothers in Christ.

1 John 1:3 A person cannot have true spiritual fellowship with Christians until he has heard the facts of the gospel and has acted upon those facts by accepting Christ as his Savior.

Revelation 19:10 The brethren are defined as those who have the testimony of Jesus.

John 13:30, 34, 35 Judas, who did not believe on Christ, had left the table before this command for special love among Christians was given.

John 21:23 It is clear that "brethren" as used here speaks of believers.

Acts 9:17 Saul was considered a "brother" only after he had taken Christ as his Savior.

Acts 21:17 Only those who were fellow believers were the "brethren."

1 Corinthians 7:12 In this passage the man is a believer and therefore a brother. The wife is not a believer and therefore is not included in this term.

There are three practical aspects of the brotherhood of believers. The first practical aspect is that brothers in Christ should be a *spiritual help* to each other.

Romans 12:10 Christians should love one another and should desire the advancement of their brothers rather than their own advancement.

1 Corinthians 12:26, 27 Christians should sorrow when other Christians suffer, and should rejoice when other Christians have joy.

Romans 15:30; 2 Corinthians 1:8, 11 Christian brothers are to pray for each other.

Ephesians 4:15, 16 When individual Christians become what they should be, the Church becomes what it should be. Each Christian has something to contribute to this.

Ephesians 5:21–6:9 The brotherhood of believers should be the predominant factor between Christians in all the relationships of life. This is true of husbands and wives, children and parents, servants and masters, employees and employers. In all such relationships we are also brothers and sisters. See Song of Solomon 4:9, 10, 12.

Ephesians 6:18   Christians should pray for each other and for all other Christians. The brotherhood of believers cuts across the lines of nationality, race, language, culture, social position, and geographical location.

1 Thessalonians 5:11   The two great spiritual helps which brothers in Christ should be to each other are that of comforting (encouraging) one another and edifying one another. The latter means helping other Christians to be what they should be in doctrine and life.

The second practical aspect is that brothers in Christ should be a *material help* to each other.

Acts 11:29   From the earliest days of the Church Christians gave of their material goods to help those brothers in Christ who had less materially, even those at great geographical distance.

2 Corinthians 8:4   This is one illustration of many examples given in the New Testament of Christians giving money to help other Christians in material need.

Romans 12:13; Titus 1:8; Philemon 5, 7, 22   One form of practical help is by giving hospitality.

1 John 3:17, 18   There is no use talking about Christian love if we do not help our brothers in Christ when they have material needs.

Acts 5:4   The Christians helped each other materially but they did it voluntarily. Each man kept the right of personal possession.

The third aspect is that brothers in Christ should enjoy the *fellowship and companionship* of each other.

Acts 2:42, 46 From the earliest days of the Church, the Christians had daily fellowship with each other.

Ephesians 4:1–3; Colossians 2:1, 2, True Christians should try to have fellowship together in love and peace.

Hebrews 10:25 It is the direct command of our Lord that after we have become Christians we should meet together for worship with other Christians. This was not just to be a passing thing in the early days of the Church but should continue even until Christ comes back again. This verse says we should be especially careful to keep this command as we come toward the time of the second coming of Christ. If we have accepted Christ as our Savior, we have the responsibility to search out a Bible-believing group of God's people, where there is right doctrine, love, and community, and worship with them. We should not join ourselves to just any group that calls itself Christian, but one where the preaching is truly biblical and where discipline is maintained as the Bible directs, so that the external body of believers is kept from false life and false doctrine.

We have seen that the brotherhood of believers crosses all the lines of space. It also crosses all the lines of time.

Hebrews 12:22, 23 This brotherhood includes not just Christians on the earth today, but Christians who are in heaven.

18 / NEVER LOST AGAIN

We have seen that salvation immediately includes justification and new relationship. Now we come to a third consideration: once we accept Christ as Savior, we will never be lost again.

Romans 8:31–34 We will never be lost again, because of the perfection of Christ's priestly work for us. The ground of our salvation is not our good works in the past, present, or future, but the perfect work of Christ. Christ's perfect priestly work includes two things: his perfect death and his perfect intercession for us now.

Hebrews 7:25 This one passage reminds us of everything we studied under the heading "Christ's work as priest," including his present intercession for us. You will remember that this verse teaches that the Lord saves us both completely and forever. The Christian could be lost again only if Christ failed as a priest.

Romans 8:28–30; Ephesians 1:3–7 After becoming Christians by accepting Christ, we learn that God the Father has chosen us. The Christian could be lost again only if the first person of the Trinity, the Father, failed.

Ephesians 1:13, 14 In days gone by when a man bought some land, he was given a handful of earth (an earnest) to signify that all the land was his. The fact that the Holy Spirit now lives in us is a promise (an earnest) that one day we will have all the benefits of salvation. We will not be lost again.

Ephesians 4:30 In past centuries a king would seal a document with wax and then mark the wax with his ring. No man then dared to break this seal except under the authority of the king. This passage says that God himself has sealed us with the indwelling Holy Spirit unto the day of redemption, that is, until the day in which we will receive all the benefits of redemption. A rebel might break a human king's seal, but nothing which God has created can break the seal of God.

Romans 8:26   When we do not know how to pray for ourselves as we should, the indwelling Spirit prays for us. The Christian could be lost again only if the Holy Spirit failed.

John 10:27–29   Christ says that when we accept him as our Savior, we have eternal life. Eternal life could be no shorter than eternity. Christ says we shall never perish; "never" can only mean "never." Christ says that nothing can pluck us out his hand or the Father's hand. It's not that we hold fast to God; he holds fast to us.

Romans 8:35–39   Here God says specifically that no created thing can separate us from himself after we have come through Jesus Christ.

Philippians 1:6   "The day of Jesus Christ" is Christ's second coming, when we will receive the full benefits of salvation.

1 John 4:13; 5:13   Notice the use of the word "know." God wants us to have the assurance that we are his and will be forever.

2 Timothy 4:7, 8   Paul had this assurance.

Romans 8:15, 16   The assurance that we are God's children and that we will be his forever is one of the good things God means us to have after we have accepted Christ as

Savior. Not all who are true Christians have this assurance, but if they do not, they have not taken advantage of one of the riches in Christ Jesus which it is their privilege to have right now.

John 3:36 "He that believes on the Son has everlasting life." If you know that you have believed in Christ for your salvation and are not trusting in your own moral or religious works, then you have the express promise of God that you do have everlasting life, *now and forever.*

19 / SANCTIFICATION (A)

We have seen that once we accept Christ as Savior, we are justified. We enter into a new relationship with each of the three persons of the Trinity. We will never be lost again. In this study we begin to consider another part of our salvation — sanctification. While justification deals with the past (once I have become a Christian), sanctification deals with the present. It has to do with the power of sin in the Christian's life. Justification is the same for all Christians, but obviously sanctification has proceeded further in some Christians than in others. For a book-length study of the subject of sanctification, see the author's book *True Spirituality,* Tyndale House Publishers.

Romans 8:29, 30 Salvation is not a blank from the time we are justified until we reach heaven. Rather, it is a flowing stream involving the past (when we became Christians), the present, and into the future. If we have truly taken Christ as our Savior, this has many implications for our present lives, including the fact that our lives should show that we are Christ's.

Colossians 3:1–3 Once we have accepted Christ as personal Savior, it should make a difference in the lives we live.

John 15:1–5 If a man is truly a Christian, there will be spiritual fruit in his life.

1 Thessalonians 5:23; Hebrews 13:20, 21 God the Father is active in our sanctification.

Ephesians 5:25, 26; Titus 2:11–14 So is God the Son.

1 Corinthians 6:11; 2 Corinthians 3:18; 2 Thessalonians 2:13 God the Holy Spirit is active in our sanctification.

Romans 12:1–19; 2 Corinthians 7:1; Colossians 3:1–4:6 These are just a few of the commands given in the Bible as to how we should walk in this life. As Christians, God's law is our rule of life. In such passages as these, God tells us what conforms to his character and what pleases him. Being Christians should make a difference in every aspect of our lives.

1 Corinthians 6:20 We were saved by faith, not by good works. But after we are saved, we should show forth our gratitude in our lives by good works.

Matthew 22:37, 38; Revelation 2:1–5 The only proper basic motive for desiring to get over our sins and to grow spiritually is our love for God. Fear of getting caught, etc. will not do. We are to live a Christian life because we love the Lord and wish to glorify him.

John 15:8 When a believer sins, he is not glorifying the heavenly Father as he should.

Philippians 1:20 When a believer sins, he is not showing forth the glory of Christ in this present life, as a reborn man should.

Romans 8:8; Galatians 5:16–25; Ephesians 5:18; 4:30; 1 Thessalonians 5:19 When a person accepts Christ as Savior, he is indwelt by the Holy Spirit immediately and from then on. But when a believer sins, he is walking after the flesh and not after the Spirit. He is grieving (making sad) and quenching the Holy Spirit who indwells him.

1 John 1:3, 7; 2:1 When a Christian sins, he does not lose his salvation. The blood of Christ is enough to cover the sin, and Christ, on the right hand of the Father, intercedes for the Christian. But a Christian does break his fellowship with God when he sins. If a child is disobedient, he does not cease being a child of his parent. But the joy of the child-parent relationship is gone. As long as our fellowship with our heavenly Father is broken because of sin, we cannot expect spiritual power or joy.

Hebrews 12:5–11 When a believer sins, God chastens him in this life, even as a loving human parent chastens his child. God does not do this to punish us, for our sins were punished once for all on Calvary, but to bring forth the peaceable fruit of righteousness in our lives. However, remember that all the troubles of life are not necessarily the result of personal sin. For example, consider the trials of Job.

2 Corinthians 5:9, 10; 1 Corinthians 3:11–15; Luke 19:11–27 In the future life, the Christian will receive rewards, which will depend on the life now lived after he has become a Christian. In Luke notice the distinction between the Christians (servants), who receive rewards, and the non-Christians (citizens and enemies), who are put aside.

1 Corinthians 11:31, 32   When a Christian sins, his fellowship with God can be restored. The first thing necessary is to acknowledge that the thing which we have done is sin. As surely as God the Father is our Father, if we do not do this he will chasten us.

1 John 1:9   After self-judgment, acknowledging his sin to be sin, the believer must confess his sin to God — not to a priest or any other man, but directly to God. He is our Father, and in prayer we can come into his presence at any time. We must bring the specific sin under the finished work of Christ. Now our fellowship with God is restored. After this confession, the matter is finished, unless I have injured men by my sin. Then, of course, if I am repentant, I will desire to make restitution.

1 John 1:8   The process of sanctification goes on until death. By God's grace, the Christian always has new ground to win for Christ.

20 / SANCTIFICATION (B)

Matthew 5:48   While we will always have new ground to gain for Christ in our lives, our standard for every moment must be no lower than God's command, that is, perfection.

Ephesians 4:12, 13; 2 Peter 3:18   While it is a comforting truth that when a Christian sins he can confess his sins and have his fellowship with God restored, yet our Christian lives should be something more than always sinning and confessing the same old sins.

Romans 6:1–19 If we have partaken of the benefit of Christ's death for justification, we should also be partakers of the power of his life, so that we should no longer serve sin. As we yield to Christ at this one moment, he will bring forth his fruit through us.

2 Corinthians 13:14 As seen in our studies of the "new relationship" we have with God, we have a personal relationship with each of the three members of the Trinity. Our relationship is never mechanical and not primarily legal. It is personal and vital. God the Father is my Father; I am united and identified with God the Son; God the Holy Spirit dwells within me. The Bible tells us that this threefold relationship is a present fact, just as it tells us that justification and heaven are facts.

We have seen that once we are saved, we are always saved, but that some Christians do not have this confidence, simply because they have never realized what the Bible teaches concerning assurance or, knowing the facts, they have not rested on them.

It is also possible to be a Christian and yet not take advantage of what our vital relationship with the three persons of the Trinity should mean in living a Christian life. We must first intellectually realize the fact of our vital relationship with the triune God and then in faith begin to act upon that realization. At this point I would urge you to glance again over the three studies on our "new relationship" with the Father, Son, and Holy Spirit.

Ephesians 3:14–19; 2 Corinthians 12:9 It is not my

weakness but the triune God's strength that counts.

1 John 5:3–5 The victory that overcomes the world is our faith. (It is not that the ground is our faith; in sanctification, as in justification, the only ground is the perfect, finished work of Christ.) The Bible tells us both the fact of justification and the fact of our present vital relationship with the Trinity. But mere intellectual acceptance is not enough in either case. Knowing the facts, we must rest upon them in faith. Justification is an *act;* I throw myself on Christ as Savior once, and God declares me justified forever. Sanctification is a *process* which begins when I take Christ as my Savior and continues until I die. Thus, for my daily walk as a Christian, I must by God's grace rest in faith upon my present vital relationship with the three persons of the Trinity for every moment of my life. In both justification and sanctification I must see that I cannot keep God's law in my own strength. Therefore for my justification I must have rested in faith in Christ as my Savior; in sanctification moment by moment I must throw myself upon the fact of my present vital relationship with Father, Son, and Holy Spirit. The Bible tells me that this vital relationship is a fact. Through faith I lay hold of this fact for this one moment, and all of life is only a succession of moments — one moment at a time. Thus, by God's grace, "his commandments are not grievous." And, by God's grace, I may have spiritual power and the Lord will be my song.

21 / SANCTIFICATION (C)

1 Peter 2:2; John 17:17; Acts 17:11; Acts 20:32; Ephesians 5:26; 2 Timothy 2:15 There are four practices which help us greatly to grow spiritually. The first is the study of the Bible, which is the Word of God.

Philippians 4:6; 1 Thessalonians 5:17 The second is prayer. We should cultivate the habit of two types of prayer:

(a) Special times of prayer, such as morning and evening, grace at meals, and from time to time, special days of prayer.

(b) Praying constantly as we go about our daily tasks.

Acts 1:8 The third is witnessing for Christ. This command is to all Christians. You can do your part, you can be a "teller," no matter where the Lord places you in life.

Hebrews 10:24, 25; Acts 2:46, 47 The fourth is regular attendance at a Bible-believing church. As we saw under "The Brotherhood of Believers," this does not mean just any church or group, but one which is true to the Word of God — that has an orthodoxy of doctrine and an orthodoxy of love and community. In connection with our regular attendance with the Lord's people, we also have the privilege of partaking in the Lord's Supper.

It is wonderful to know that we are justified and that we will be in heaven. But our present desire should be to glorify the triune God because we love the Father, because we love the Son, because we love the Holy Spirit.

22 / GLORIFICATION AT DEATH

As we have previously seen, our salvation includes things past, present, and future. If we have accepted Christ as Savior, justification (God's declaration that our guilt is covered) is past. Sanctification deals with the present. Glorification is that which comes to a Christian at death and afterwards.

2 Thessalonians 1:4–10 The Bible speaks here of that which all of us can observe in the world about us. It is obvious that the accounts of life are not balanced in this life. Christians are often persecuted, while wicked men seem to prosper. This passage of Scripture teaches that the very fact these inequalities take place in this life proves that there will be a judgment by God, who is perfectly just. The books will be balanced.

John 3:36 When we accept Christ as our Savior, we are promised not a salvation which terminates with this life, but an everlasting salvation.

Psalm 23:6 The word "house" here could be translated "household." Thus, what this verse teaches is that once I have taken Christ as my Savior, I will be in the household of God — not only for this life but for eternity. To the Christian, death is like going from one room to another in the same house.

Ecclesiastes 12:7 Notice the clear distinction made here between the body and the soul at death. Physical death is the separation of soul and body.

Luke 23:39–43 When the Christian dies, the body goes into the grave but the soul is immediately with Christ.

Acts 7:54–59 At the Christian's death the soul is immediately in Christ's presence.

2 Corinthians 5:6, 8 For the Christian, death is not something to fear. It brings us entrance into that which is better than we now possess.

Luke 9:28–36 Moses died and was buried about 1500 years before this event took place. But the disciples recognized him, even though they had never seen him and even though, as far as we know, his body was still in the grave. When we die, we can expect to know our loved ones and other Christians, even though their bodies are still in their graves.

Acts 7:59, 60 Stephen's soul was immediately with Christ, but his body fell asleep.

1 Thessalonians 4:14 When a Christian dies and his soul is immediately with Christ, the Bible speaks of his body as asleep in Christ. The Lord is interested in our bodies as well as our souls.

23 / GLORIFICATION AT THE RESURRECTION

Genesis 2:7 God made our bodies as well as our souls.

Genesis 3:1–20 Man's fall into sin involved the complete man, both body and soul. Because man sinned, three deaths came upon him. Spiritual death (separation from God) came immediately. Physical death is what we usually speak of as "death." Eternal death will come at the final judgment. When we take Christ as our Savior, the first and third of the above three deaths are finished for us. Our fellowship with God is restored and our sins have been punished once for all on Calvary. The second death, the separation of soul and body at death, has yet to be dealt with.

Romans 8:23 We have the "firstfruits of the Spirit," but there is still the last step to be realized — the "redemption" of the Christian's body.

1 Corinthians 15:12–26 As Christ rose physically from the dead, so the bodies of Christians will also be raised physically. When this happens, our redemption, our salvation, will be complete. Just as God made the whole man and the whole man fell, so the whole man will be redeemed.

1 Corinthians 15:52–58; 1 Thessalonians 4:13, 14 The bodies of Christians who have died ("them which are asleep") will be raised from the dead when Christ comes back again.

1 Corinthians 15:51, 52; 1 Thessalonians 4:13–18 These verses show us that those Christians still alive when Christ comes back will not go through death. Their bodies will be changed in a twinkling of an eye — as fast as it takes to wink. They will pass immediately from this present life to full glorification.

Philippians 3:20, 21; 1 John 3:2 The glorified bodies of all Christians (whether they have died and have been raised again or have been changed in a twinkling of an eye) will be like Christ's body after his resurrection.

John 20:26 After his resurrection, Christ's body could pass through closed doors. After our glorification, we will be able to do the same.

Luke 24:36–43 After his resurrection Christ could and did eat. After our glorification we will do the same.

John 20:27, 28 The conclusion of each of the four Gospels and the beginning of Acts tell us what a wonderful body

Christ had after his resurrection. But it is clear from this verse and others that this was not a new body that Christ had after his resurrection, but the same body which he had before his death and at his death. After our glorification, we will have the same bodies as we have now, but glorified. They will be changed bodies, glorified bodies, but the same bodies.

IV. THINGS OF THE FUTURE

In this series of Bible studies, we have considered three large sections: "God," "God's Dealing with Man," and "Salvation." Now we will finish with a short section of two studies on the things of the future. Of course, what we have already studied of the Christian's glorification at death and at the resurrection is also future for us.

In this chapter we will look at the external world and the people of God.

Luke 18:8; 17:26–30 The world is not going to get better and better. The Christian's hope is not the gradual betterment of the world but that Christ is coming back again.

Acts 1:10, 11; Mark 13:26; 1 Corinthians 15:23; Philippians 3:20, 21; 1 Thessalonians 1:10; 2:19; 3:13; 4:14, 16, 17; 2 Thessalonians 1:7; 1 Timothy 6:14; Titus 2: 12, 13; 2 Peter 3:3–14; Revelation 1:7, 8 The fact of Christ's coming again is clearly stated.

Acts 1:6–9; Matthew 24:36; 25:13; Mark 13:32, 33; Luke 12:35–40 The time of Christ's return is not given. These verses teach us to not set times, saying we know when he is coming. On the other hand, they tell us that Christ may come at any time. The Christian should be constantly awaiting him. The command is to "watch."

1 Thessalonians 3:13; 4:13–17 True Christians, those who have put their faith in Christ as Savior, shall be caught up to meet Christ in the air and then come with him. It is at this time that the bodies of Christians who have died will be raised from the dead and that living Christians will be glorified in a twinkling of an eye.

Matthew 24:36–44; Luke 17:26–30, 34–36; 21:36; Isaiah 26:19–21 Noah was out of danger in the ark before the flood came. Lot was safe before the destruction of Sodom began. It would seem that in the same way, true Christians will be taken out of danger before God's wrath is poured out upon the earth. Some Christians will be sleeping when they are taken, some will be awake. But all true Christians will be taken. The unsaved will be left.

Matthew 25:1–13 In this parable the Lord shows that not even all of those who are church members will be taken. Church members who have not put their personal faith in Christ as their Savior, and therefore are not indwelt by the Holy Spirit (no oil in their lamps), will be left.

2 Thessalonians 2:1–12; Revelation 13:1–18 Before Christ's coming visibly and in glory with his saints, there will be a period of great apostasy with a dictator, called the "Antichrist," ruling the world. He is completely opposite and opposed to Christ, completely subservient to

Satan, the "dragon." He will control governmental and economic life and will be worshiped as God.

Jeremiah 30:1-7; Revelation 7:4-8 During this period, God will deal again with the Jews as a nation. They will be back in Palestine. As the Antichrist persecutes them, this will be the time of "Jacob's trouble."

Revelation 6:1-17; 8:7-9:21; 11:13, 14; 15:1 God's wrath is poured out upon the earth during this period.

Revelation 16:13-16; 19:11-21 Here Christ comes visibly and in glory. He overthrows the assembled might of the world organized against him by the Antichrist and Satan. This is the battle of Armageddon. This is not just a great war between nations; it is the final confrontation between the world's might under Antichrist and Satan, and Christ and the glorified Christians.

Revelation 20:1-6; Romans 8:19-23; Isaiah 11:1-10 The devil is shut up, and Christ rules the earth for a thousand years. The bodies of all true Christians will have been redeemed and glorified. Then the curse which God put upon the earth (Genesis 3:17, 18) because of man's sin will be removed. The world will, during this period, then be normal again, that is, as God made it.

Revelation 20:6; Luke 19:11-27 The Christians (servants) will reign with Christ during this period. Apparently our place of service in that time will be conditioned by our faithfulness in this present time.

Isaiah 11:10-12:6; Jeremiah 30:7-9; Zechariah 12:8-10; 13:6; 14:16-21; Romans 11:25-29 When Christ comes back in glory, the Jews will see him as the true

Messiah whom they, as a nation, rejected; and they will believe on him.

Revelation 20:7–15 At the end of the thousand years, Satan will be loosed for a little while. There will be a final revolt against Christ, and the judgment of the lost will take place.

Revelation 21:1–22:5 There will be a new heaven, a new earth, and a heavenly city. It is definite, so that this passage can state the size of the heavenly city, that from which it is constructed, that from which its foundations, gates, and streets are made. It is an objective reality. It is eternal — forever and ever, without end.

> "When we've been there ten thousand years,
> Bright shining as the sun,
> We've no less days to sing God's praise,
> Than when we first begun."

25 / THE LOST

We have studied the present and future of those who have accepted God's gift of salvation by accepting Christ as Savior. This final study is the other side.

Revelation 19:20 This describes the end of the Antichrist and also the false religious head who led in the worship of him.

Revelation 20:10; Isaiah 14:9–17 Originally created as the angel Lucifer (son of the morning), Satan revolted against God. This is his end.

Jude 6; 2 Peter 2:4; 1 Corinthians 6:3; Matthew 8:28, 29

This is the end of the angels who followed Satan in his revolt.

Romans 2:5, 6; 2 Thessalonians 1:4–9 There is a day of judgment for men and women who follow Satan in his revolt.

Daniel 12:2; John 5:28, 29; Acts 24:15 There will be a future physical resurrection of the lost.

Revelation 20:5, 6 The physical resurrection of the lost takes place a thousand years after the physical resurrection of the Christians. All Christians are raised in the first resurrection, and they need not fear the "second death," the condemnation of the final judgment. Either a person must be twice-born (natural birth and the new birth when he takes Christ as Savior), or he must die twice (the natural death and eternal judgment).

John 8:44; Matthew 25:41, 46; Revelation 20:11–15 The end of the lost is the same as that of the devil and the angels who follow him. As the complete man (body and soul) of those who put their faith in Christ is redeemed, so the complete man (body and soul) of those who do not accept God's gift of salvation is judged. Hell is prepared for the devil and his angels, and the result of following him is to end up in the same place.

Matthew 3:12; 5:22; 8:12; 13:42, 50; 22:13; 25:30; Mark 9:43–48; Colossians 3:6; 2 Peter 2:17; 3:7; Revelation 19:20; 20:15. In these and many other verses the Bible speaks of this place. Notice how much of this is given by Christ himself, the one who came and died so that men might escape this by accepting him as Savior.

Luke 12:48 There are degrees of judgment. As there is a

believer's judgment, there are also degrees of judgment of the lost. There is a balancing of the books on both sides of the chasm.

Matthew 18:8; 25:41, 46; 2 Thessalonians 1:9; Jude 13; Revelation 20:10 The same words are used in the original Greek for the eternal quality of the future of the lost as are used for the eternal quality of the future of the redeemed. The two stand parallel.

In concluding this sober study, what should be in our minds?

Romans 5:8, 9; Ephesians 2:1–9; 1 Thessalonians 1:10 If we are Christians, remember that this is what we have been saved from by the death of Christ on Calvary. He suffered there infinitely, so that we might not be separated from God everlastingly.

Matthew 28:19, 20; Romans 10:13–15; Revelation 22:17 If we are Christians, in the light of this study, we should give ourselves completely to the task which Christ has given to the Church in this age — telling others the content of the gospel.

Matthew 11:28–30 If you have not yet taken Christ as your Savior, if you are not a Christian, the triune God invites you to come and accept God's free gift of salvation by accepting Christ as Savior.

John 3:36 If you are not a Christian, you are here told once more that the judgment of God is upon you. But this same verse tells you as clearly as can be put into human language that there is only one thing necessary to have that other everlasting — everlasting life, immediately and without end.